PAPA

Prell Davis

Illustrated by: Elexiss Allison

ISBN: Softcover   978-1-4990-3758-6
       Hardcover   978-1-4990-3757-9
       EBook   978-1-4990-3759-3

Rev. date: 06/18/2014

To order additional copies of this book, contact:
Xlibris LLC
1-888-795-4274
www.Xlibris.com
Orders@Xlibris.com

Dedication

In memory of my Uncle Benny D. Hampton
Dedicated to my Aunt Edna H. Hampton, I will hold
you in my heart always.
To my dad, William Moore, I will always cherish our
conversations and time spent together.

To Papa and Nana's grandchildren: Elexiss, Aidan,
Jada, Dana, Elijah, and Micah, always remember what
they have taught you.

Acknowledgements

To my Father God,
thank you for helping me through this process.
To Davis Photography,
thank you for the vibrant photographs.
A special thanks to Elexiss Allison for her colorful and
beautiful illustrations.

I have a
grandfather.
His name is Benny
Douglas Hampton,
but we call him
Papa.

When Papa watches
television, he loves to
eat popcorn. He says
"shake the popcorn
in your hand and then
put it in your mouth
and eat it."

Sometimes he takes us for a ride in "Big Red". Big Red is a 1980 Ford truck that Papa inherited from his father.

After school Papa likes to
help us with
our homework.
He always tells us to
"never stop learning."

Whenever he goes places,
Papa seems to make
friends with everyone
he meets.

When we are
playing outside,
Papa teaches us how to
ride our bikes.

On warm days,
Papa likes to cook outside
for our family.
Everyone loves to eat his
grilled food.

If we are sad,
Papa kisses us on our
foreheads and says,
"everything will work out
ok pumpkins."

Papa enjoys spending time with his grandchildren, and we love being around him. We will always love Papa Benny, because he showed us how you enjoy life.

Printed in the United States
by Baker & Taylor Publisher Services